ASTROLOGICAL CYCLES

ASTROLOGICAL CYCLES

&

THE LIFE CRISIS PERIODS

by

JOHN TOWNLEY

SAMUEL WEISER INC.   NEW YORK

First published 1977
Second printing 1978

Samuel Weiser, Inc.
740 Broadway
New York, N.Y. 10003

ISBN 0-87728-359-1

Printed in the
United States of America
by Noble Offset Printers, Inc.
New York City

TABLE OF CONTENTS

*. . . . To Christine; my wife, my lover,
my business partner, and my best friend.. . . .*

INTRODUCTION

CYCLE (si kil) n. 1. A time interval in which a characteristic, especially a regularly repeated, event or sequence of events occurs. 2.a. A single complete execution of a periodically repeated phenomenon. b. A periodically repeated sequence of events. 3. The orbit of a celestial body. 4. A long period of time; an age; eon. . .'' — The American Heritage Dictionary, © 1969

There is nothing quite so basic to human experience as the cycle. We order ourselves and, indeed, keep our sanity sheerly by the knowledge and use of countless different kinds of cycles. Our heartbeat, brainwaves, and the rhythm of our breathing are the three signs of life itself — when these three disappear, clinical death has occurred. Our entire mental grasp of the world depends on cycles — if events did not recur, there could be no graspable, structured universe.

The very multiplicity of cycles makes any unified approach to the subject very nearly impossible. There are song cycles, weather cycles, seasonal cycles, crop cycles, economic cycles, civilization cycles, endocrine cycles, synodic cycles, war cycles, migration cycles, fashion cycles, popular and folk music cycles, depression cycles, unicycles, bicycles, tricycles, and motorcycles, just to scratch the surface of the problem. The word is derived from the ancient Greek ''kuklos'', meaning circle. One profitable and time-honored approach to the study of cycles is the study of the largest circles man has traditionally dealt with – the orbits of the planets. The attempt to correlate these ''circles'' with the innumerable cyclic events on earth has long gone by the name astrology.

Over the nearly three thousand years that astrology as we know it has been in existence, reams of literature have been written on the possible implications of the combined influences of the planets and their varying cycles upon human behaviour. Astrologers and astronomers, mystics and scientists, believers and unbelievers — all have had more than a few words to say upon the subject. Recently, for the first time ever, modern science is beginning to commit some effort to explore the subject, and the coming decades should shed tremendous new light upon the area. Meanwhile, on a day-to-day basis, astrologers continue to use a mass of traditional beliefs based on the experience and writing of those that came before them.

It is essentially these traditions and beliefs, at least as they display themselves as repeating cyclic phenomena, that this book is about. The various methods of interpretation of the natal horoscope, about which there are many excellent works, will not be discussed, but rather the repeating occurrences both astronomical and human that provide the background for interpretation will be described. We are concerned here with the regular rhythm of event-patterns that individuals face, according to the dictates of their horoscope. All persons, at least as described by their horoscopes, are special and individual, and the interpretation of these individualities is the responsibility of the private astrologer. However, the mathematics of celestial mechanics and traditional astrology indicate that *everyone* must experience certain fixed planetary cycles to which each individual may respond slightly differently, but which nonetheless retain their specific description and flavor. This book describes and, hopefully, helps to clarify these experiences that we all must share not only because we are human, but because we happen to live on this planet.

ASTROLOGICAL CYCLES

Diurnal Cycles

OUR ALARM CLOCK begins the shortest and most primary of astrological cycles. As the sun bursts over the eastern horizon, schoolchildren are dragged out of bed, early birds swallow their worms, partygoers nurse their hangovers, and another local 24-hour rotational cycle of the earth is begun.

As far as our bodies are concerned, this is the most important cycle we experience. Almost all of our physical functions are more or less synchronized with it, and we suffer discomfort if they are interrupted. TV commercials that promote remedies for "irregularity" are a testament to this, and any parent knows that the only way to toilet-train a toddler is by maintaining a careful daily schedule. Early risers will wake up every morning at the same time without an alarm, and when Sunday morning rolls around sleeping late is nearly impossible. When vacation time tries to interrupt this morning custom, one wakes up with a feeling that there's work to be done and then rolls over, not entirely in relief, knowing that there isn't.

The last two decades has seen a lot of medical research on the subject of diurnal, or "circadian," rhythms. A good deal of publicity has been given to the problem of "jet-lag" in the case of travellers and particularly pilots, whose operations may be hindered by becoming artificially "out-of-sync" with normal diurnal rhythms. The problem is no less critical in a hospital ward, where different dosages of medicines are given at different times of day.

These rhythms of highs and lows during a 24-hour period vary with the individual, but in mass studies certain common patterns tend to emerge. The oldest and most familiar of these is the 9-to-5 worker's rhythm: low in the morning, high around lunchtime, and low around four in the afternoon. This familiar rhythm spawned what has become an integral part of an office worker's day — the coffee break, the introduction of which was intended to relieve those low points and foster greater working efficiency. Dr. Pepper's old advertising slogan (before it was bought by Coca-Cola), "10-2-4", was also a product of this rhythm, harboring the suggestion that you drink a bottle of the caffeinated beverage at both the lows and the peak of the workday cycle.

Not all of us are privileged at be awake enough in the morning to experiece any kind of high or low at all, however, and this well-known fact led to some interesting research and conclusions by Dr. Nathaniel Kleitman, a physiologist and sleep-researcher at the University of Chicago. His theory is as follows: there are two basic personality types, morning and evening. Morning people are up bright and early and tend to be more conservative and less creative types. Evening people abhor the sunrise and are hardly really functioning before noon, but tend toward the more creative and revolutionary and often work far into the night.

He cites as famous examples presidents Harry Truman and Franklin D. Roosevelt. Truman was always up at the crack of dawn before the rest of his staff, but he was essentially a countrified old-timer quite fixed in his ways and not a particularly innovative president. F.D.R., on the other hand, conducted most of his morning business from bed, worked far into the evening, and was certainly this century's most radical and innovative president to date.

Dr. Kleitman further notes that persons in the so-called "creative" professions — writers, actors, artists, musicians — tend to be evening types. Of particular note as well is the governmental habit in Soviet Russia of conducting business well into the evening hours, a habit inherited from their original revolutionary Bolsheviks that has not yet worn off. This could as well be a nice argument in favor of the Gemini-rising chart for the U.S. Declaration of Independence, placing the finalizing of the document in the wee hours of the morning. Over its 200-year history, however, this country has lost much of its revolutionary flavor and is mostly made up of morning types these days.

It would be well for unions and employers to recognize these rather self-evident personality rhythms — some people really do work better at night, and the workaday life might be a lot easier and more profitable for everyone concerned if this were taken into account. It is one of the strongest, though seldom quoted, arguments for the staggered workday.

A good astrological picture of these personality types has yet to present itself. Morning and evening types seem to be equally likely to have planets above or below the horizon, masculine and feminine signs, and other seemingly likely explanations. Considerable research will be needed in order to uncover a convincing signature.

◆ ◆ ◆

But personality types aside, there is a regular rhythm of the rising and setting of the sun, moon, and planets each day that appears to have an effect on human events concomitant with them. Their meaning in astrology has been unraveled primarily by the technique of casting charts for various events and finding out what planets are rising, setting, or culminating at the time.

The greatest effect is noticed when a planet is rising, somewhat less but still noticable when culminating, and negative or reversed when setting. Specifically:

The Sun — By definition, the sun rises only in the morning and signifies beginnings in a very basic and primal way. Beginnings are easier (particularly for evening types) with the sun culminating at the midheaven or slightly before it, to get maximum career effect and ensure that a sunny reputation will evolve from the matter. When choosing, or interpreting the time of any event, the sun's house position, not just rising or culminating, is of the utmost importance as it indicates the most basic nature of the event.

The Moon — The moon when rising indicates sudden change, fluctuation, and motion, sometimes deceit or surprise. For instance, the 1973 October Arab-Israeli war was begun with the moon and Jupiter exactly rising (overwhelming and sudden surprise), with the sun in the 8th house (death, destruction) *exactly besieged* between Uranus and Pluto (a two-front war). This does not mean you may expect an attack each day when the moon rises, but it does tend to be a pretty shifty time of day. The moon culminating, on the other hand, indicates events that will likely be publicized, so that the native could suffer scandal or enjoy great fame, depending on the rest of the chart and the nature of the event.

Mercury — Mercury must, of neccessity, rise within about two hours before or after sunrise. It doesn't generally indicate gross physical events, but rather tends to herald new ideas, sudden flashes of inspiration, and the like, mostly for morning types. The same effect for evening types is more often brought about by Uranus, as they usually are asleep when Mercury rises. Mercury culminating is rather like a combination of sun and moon — an idea whose time has come and that either has or will achieve reputation abroad.

Venus — Like Mercury, Venus is tied to the sun from our point of view and must rise within three hours of sunrise. For the morning personality its rise often accompanies bursts of creativity, but for everyone it is definitely associated with early morning erotic dreaming. Culminating, it is good for efforts that bring a pleasant reputation and monetary investments and returns. As the evening star, Venus setting has always been associated with good fortune in love, particularly when pursued later that evening when it, along with the sun, proceeds through the fifth house.

Mars — In natal horoscopes, according to Michel Gauquelin's statistical research, rising or culminating Mars is to be found especially in the charts of athletes. Certainly its daily rise is often associated with physical effort and extra feats of strength. Often, however, it may be accompanied by altercations, arguments, or even blows if the situation warrants. Throughout tradition it has seldom been looked upon favorably except in contests of strength and the like. It apparently has the effect of putting too much energy into most situations. Culminating, the effect is more general and causes occurrences that receive too much attention.

Jupiter — As in the case of the Arab-Israeli war, Jupiter rising tends to make events seem a bit overwhelming. It is a likely time for overly heavy sales pitches, tall tales, and other diverse bits of hyperbole that spice up ordinarily drab reality. Events occurring at this time deserve to be taken with a grain or two of salt, as the final outcome is not always everything that is promised at the beginning. Culminating, Jupiter is the most benefic of planets and runs along with events that seem to have unlimited potential.

Saturn — Saturn rising has had a bit of a bad name throughout astrological history, being associated with loss, accidents, imprisonment, and the like. It can equally well accompany events of a more positive nature concerning older people, the implementing of older ideas and the establishment, or the achieving of long-range goals. It can display as simple a reaction as the sudden cessation of conversation in a room, or as common a phenomenon as running out of gas (literally or figuratively). Culminating, it tends to bring stoppage in general, except in cases of enshrinement or entombment where the crystalizing nature of the planet is displayed in a socially favorable way.

Uranus — Uranus rising certainly brings more excitement and tension than any other planet. On the down side, it can accompany accidents, sudden injury, or violent arguments, but its positive side brings revolutionary change, happy surprises, and sudden inspiration. Its effect is always unpredictable, so it's a good time of day to expect the unexpected. Culminating, it brings events that tend to be misinterpreted continually by the public at large.

Neptune — As Neptune climbs over the horizon, all kinds of uncertain events are likely to occur. Wrong numbers, incorrectly relayed messages, unexplainable (and pointless) apprehension, among other Neptunian occurrences, take place. Within a few minutes, usually, the problem is cleared up, but meanwhile the imagination runs rampant concerning what might be the implications of the misunderstanding. On the creative side, it can mark individual moments of aesthetic realization or religious meditation, but not that often in a group situation. Culminating, it brings events no one ever really can correctly interpret or understand.

Pluto —Aside from its traditional association with deaths, Pluto is often found rising when someone is trying to force his will upon another, either subtly or by outright force. In a marriage, it's a great time for effective henpecking or other personality power-games. In the deepest positive sense, it can be a time of religious revelation and better understanding of the nature of the life-death process, but with most of us these occasions are rare. Culminating, it indicates events that are spoken of darkly or are thought to be of a worrisome nature.

◆ ◆ ◆

Just as most of our time on earth is spent in fairly commonplace and unnoteworthy activities, the times that the different planets rise each day will not always mark anything of great importance. What is notable, however, is how often the appropriate planet is rising when important events do happen.

Keeping daily track of when each planet rises would be an unprofitably tedious task of calculation for the average person. However, there is often help available coming from seemingly unlikely quarters. The *New York Times* every day carries the rising and setting times of the sun, moon, and visible planets (excluding Uranus, Neptune, and Pluto), as do many other papers. Similar data is available in various local and national yearly almanacs. Thus, with no effort at all, anyone can keep an eye on the rising times of various planets and test out these hypotheses for himself and hopefully utilize the possibilities that they suggest.

It is strongly suggested, however, that such data be used for observation and understanding only and not too certainly as a basis for specific action. The possibility that any given planet rising will bring well, ill, or nothing at all are intimately enlaced with other planetary positions in traditional astrology and should not be judged alone.

The Planetary Hours

No discussion of diurnal planetary cycles would be complete without a mention of the oldest method of viewing them, a system that dates back to ancient Egypt but which is mostly out of use today. In those early times, only the seven visible heavenly bodies were known to astrologers, and they were arranged in an order based on their apparent velocities: Saturn, Jupiter, Mars, Sun, Venus, Mercury, Moon. In order, each hour of the 24-hour day was given the rulership of one of the seven. Thus, if we begin with Saturn ruling the first hour, in rotation it would rule the 8th, 15th, and 22nd. In order, then, Jupiter would rule the 23rd, Mars the 24th, the Sun the 1st (the following day), and so on. The days of the week came to be known for the planetary hour that began them, resulting in our present order of the week, inherited from the Romans and further Anglo-Saxonized into our present form. In Latin: Sol (Sunday), Luna (Monday, Moon's Day), Martis (Mar's Day, changed to Tuesday after Tiu, the Germanic war god), Mercurius (Mercury's Day, changed to Wednesday after the Teutonic Woden), Jove (Jupiter's Day, renamed Thursday after Thor, the Norse thunder god), Veneris (Venus' Day, changed to Friday after Freya, Norse goddess of love).

It was believed that during the hours of the day that were under any one given ruler, events were colored accordingly. Thus, one would choose a Mars hour to attack one's enemies, a Venus hour for wooing one's lover, and so on. Although this system is generally out of use today, some astrologers still take the planetary hours into account, particularly in horary or electional matters.

Perhaps one of the reasons for its current disuse (aside from the discovery of three new planets) is the peculiar nature of the hours themselves and the difficulty of their calculation. The system was based on dividing the time from sunrise to sunset into twelve equal segments, and likewise the nighttime period of sunset to sunrise. Thus, in the summer the daytime hours were longer than the nighttime ones and varied in length from day to day. In the winter time the reverse was true, and only at the equinoxes was an hour equivalent to 60 of our standard time minutes.

This odd method of time-keeping was used in many Arab states as late as the 1930's, so birthtimes recorded then must be laboriously retranslated in order to cast a horoscope.

Personal Diurnal Cycles

Another noticeable diurnal rhythm is the rising, culminating, and setting of important degrees in an individual person's horoscope. This is considered particularly important in horary astrology (where charts are erected for the time of a question or event).

Thus, when the degree of, say, your Sun, ascendant, or midheaven is ascending or culminating, events tend to favor you or have long-range positive significance. Conversely, these degrees setting or opposite culmination indicate negative events, delays, etc. Since both peak and bottom of these occur six times daily, little in the way of overt events may be expected except occasionally — rather, these rhythms more reflect the fine tuning of more subtle daily occurrences or events that affect you that are outside of your knowledge.

Lunar Cycles

THE EFFECT OF the moon upon human behaviour has been the subject of many beliefs and much debate since the dawn of history. These days, hardly anyone will deny that the moon has *some* influence on man and his environment, but exactly what its effects are are still being hotly debated — and will be for some time to come.

We take for granted, for instance, that the interplay of earth, moon, and sun determine the cycle of the ocean's tides. This would appear to be an obvious, undeniably scientific fact. But science's acceptance of the correlation is more recent than one might think. Even Galileo, the founder of modern astronomy, believed that "any connection between the tides and the moon falls into the category of the occult."

Of course, now we know better, or at least we think we do, although there are still scientists today that believe that the tides are not caused by but are merely synchronous with the movement of the moon — a subtle distinction, but one that might apply to many of the avowed effects of astrology.

But if we think we know that the moon causes the tides, we certainly have believed it causes a lot of other events as well throughout history. For centuries farmers have planted their crops according to the phases of the moon and even laws have been enacted to govern men's actions at times of lunar stress. In England as late as the 1700's a murderer might plead "lunacy" if he had committed his crime at the time of the full moon and subsequently be given a lighter sentence.

Similarly, witches were thought to hold their Satanic services at the full moon at which they sniffed the fumes of burning deadly nightshade seeds (replete with belladonna and scopolomine) and devolved into obscene revelry. Conversely, at the dark of the moon (new moon) murderers and foul spirits were thought to be abroad — a more than likely occurrence on that darkest of nights in the month, a muggers' holiday.

This century, however, has brought a wealth of research on the subject which has served to confirm many of the old beliefs about the moon's effects.

Probably the most recent and highly-touted research is that of Dr. Arnold Lieber and his associates at the University of Miami's psychology department. He correlated the murder rates in Miami's Dade County and Cleveland's Cuyahoga County with the phases of the moon over a period of 15 years. Consistently, the murder rates peaked at the new and full moon and fell off at the quarters. According to Lieber, the resulting 15-year graph was almost exactly identical to a local tide chart for the same period.

Although the most recent research, Dr. Lieber's work was not the first in the area. An earlier report to the American Institute of Medical Climatology by the Philadelphia Police Department entitled "The Effect of the Full Moon on Human Behavior" reveals that the full moon marks a monthly peak in violent crimes and crimes with psychotic roots such as arson, destructive driving, kleptomania, and alcoholic homicide.

Dr. Lieber's explanation of this murderous phenomenon is tentative. He theorizes that the human body, made up like the earth of about 80% water, is subject to "biological tides" that result in overflows of emotional energy during monthly cycle peaks. But whatever the reason, most desk sergeants can tell you they expect a busy night at the full moon, particularly if it should coincide with a normally over-busy Saturday night.

But if more crime victims are bleeding at the full moon, so are more hospital patients undergoing surgery voluntarily. In a tabulation of 1000 tonsillectomies, Talahassee Dr. Edson J. Andrews reports (in the Journal of the Florida Medical Association) that 82% of major post-operative bleeding occurred nearer the full moon than the new, even though there were fewer admissions at that time!

It would seem that the blood runs high in more ways than one at full moon. Controller Curtis Jackson of Southern California Methodist Hospital reports that more babies are conceived on the waxing moon than on the waning. His statistics, covering 11,025 births over a period of six years (that's 38 tons of babies) show 5,975 births on the waxing moon to 5,050 on the waning, with each month's waxing births outnumbering the waning.

Earlier studies in the 1930's by Dr. W. Buehler in Germany showed a predominance of male births during the waxing moon as well, in an analysis of 33,000 births.

Conversely, deaths (in this case from TB) occurred more often 7 days after the full moon and least often 11 days before in a study by Dr. F. Petersen in Chicago. But, to date no large-scale study of deaths and lunar phases has been done.

Humans are not the only creatures to be affected by the moon. Farmers have long planted according to lunar phases, among other things, particularly favoring the period just after the full and new moon. A possible confirmation of this bucolic common sense is a 5-year New England weather study by Donald Bradly in 1962, revealing consistently heavier rainfall after the new and full moon.

Drs. H.H. Burr and F.S.C. Northrop report that the electrical potential of maple, elm, and oak wood changes with the phases of the moon — perhaps the reason farmers say shingles turn and fenceposts come up if installed on the wrong lunar phase.

Similarly, contracts for the cutting of stands of hardwood trees in South America and the Far East almost always call for cutting only during the waning moon. The reason? During the waxing moon the trees are engorged with sap which bleeds extensively during cutting and attracts the deathwatch beetle which then devastates the harvest. Thus, to preserve the crop, cut only during the waning moon.

Experiments by Prof. Frank A. Brown of Northwestern University show that animals as well respond to the moon. Screwworms change their burrowing from clockwise to counterclockwise according the lunar phases, and oysters removed far inland from the sea open and close according to what should be the times of the tides at their new location. Other experiments with fiddler crabs in a sealed environment showed they were less active when the moon was above the horizon than below, as they would have been had they been able to see it.

Most interesting of all is the finding, in an A.E.C. — sponsored report by Sandia Laboratories in New Mexico, that accident patterns among its employees over a 20-year period appeared to peak when the moon was in the opposite phase from what it was at the time of the accident victim's birth! Suddenly, simple cycle invesitigation has spilled over into pure astrology!

Lunar Cycles in Astrology

In astrology, the moon is generally considered the third most important point in the birth chart, after the sun and the ascendant. As the closest and most important to earth of all the reflective bodies in the solar system, it represents those primary qualities in the individual which are reflective, passive, and responsive in nature. Thus, while the sun may represent an individual's potential approach to a situation, the moon represents that person's likely reaction to the same situation. Thus, in a male-oriented society, the moon has often been looked at as representing the female, rather than the receptive side of the agressive-receptive polarity of every individual.

Although the moon may represent receptivity in a natal chart, as a daily transiting body it has a very active effect on the life of an individual, according to astrological experience.

Its two cycles — one of 27½ days by sign, and the other of 29½ days by phase — have a marked effect both on the individual and the environment with which he must deal from day to day.

The 29½-day phase cycle (full moon to full moon) is the most obvious and easy to deal with of the two. Any almanac and many newspapers will tell you when the phases of the moon occur, and they're worth keeping track of to help ease your way through the month. Keeping in mind the aforementioned crime statistics, it's a good idea to stay out of bars and dark streets at the full and new moon. Tension in general runs high at these times, whether at home or in the office, and many an emotional argument and hassle can be avoided if this is kept in mind.

On the other hand, in a positive emotional situation — a party, a vacation, a love affair — the full and new moon can be ridden like the crest of the wave to new heights of pleasure and enjoyment. The key to getting a positive result, in any case, is knowingly riding the wave. Attempts to too tightly control the situation usually cause things to get out of hand, rather than the other way around. Better to simply abandon yourself to the flood and let it take you where it may — ride with the tide instead of attempting to contain it.

If there is an emotional difference between the full and new moons, it is that the full is more outgoing and fun-loving, while the new is more self-contained and introspective. The new moon is as intense as the full, but much more contained.

At the moon's quarters, rational judgement is best in full play and the mind is at its clearest. It's a good time for getting everyday work done and if there is any real problem with this time it's a lack of inspiration and emotional intensity. It's a particularly good time for doing those things that might be more dangerous during the full or new moons — driving (to avoid drunk drivers), dealing with ticklish physical and emotional situations, and the like — things to do when your nerves (and those around you) are steady.

The effects of this 29½ day cycle are relatively uniform on most individuals — indeed, it is more like a tidal effect on the mass of society and biological life in general, reflected to a greater or lesser extent in individuals themselves.

But the more strictly astrological lunar cycle of 27½ days (the time it takes for the moon to complete the 360° of the tropical zodiac) is a different affair. Its effects are dependent strictly upon each individual's birth chart and vary radically from person to person.

It might seem an easy method to simply take the natal horoscope and observe the moon's transiting position during the cycle. According to traditional astrology, most events should occur when the moon touches the major occupied positions in the nativity.

Common observation reveals, however, that this is by no means always or even frequently the case. Instead, each chart seems to respond to its own unique lunar rhythm, with high spots centering most often on areas occupied by a maximum number of midpoints and lesser harmonic aspects rather than actual bodies themselves.

For the non-astrologer or student, there is an easier way of spotting the time and qualities of maximum and minimum activity in the 27½ day lunar cycle than calculating and locating dozens of these hypothetical positions. Simply locate on your calendar the periods the moon is in each sign over a period of several months (some calendars come so marked, or you can do it yourself using an ephemeris) and observe and record the type of activity that occurs throughout. This should provide you with a pretty good idea of what to expect in your own life when the moon is in varying signs — further observation should serve to correct and refine it. Such charting, based on repeated concrete experience, will serve you better than working on more hypothetical theories and will save you the endless computer sheets needed to effect an harmonic analysis that might lead you to the same conclusions. Crude, but effective.

In the end, you'll find you have one or two high and low points in the lunar month that are relatively predictable. Often, a prominent low point will be opposite your sun and a high point will be on your sun and/or your ascendant, but not always. What will appear, regardless, is a lunar rhythm that can be an aid in planning your schedule so you can rest during low points and save more important things for when you are in top-notch condition.

Another astrological function of the 27½-day cycle is a phenomenon which occurs approximately every 2 to 2½ days called the void-of-course moon. This is simply the period between the time the moon has made its last major aspect before leaving a sign and the time it enters the next sign. Based on the tenets of horary astrology, these times are considered inappropriate for important or lasting decisions and actions. It is believed that the moon, floating free and unattached by any aspect to another body, makes soggy and uncertain ground for any action that requires permanence.

As tenuous a basis for a theory as that may be, its results in practice are startling. Void-of-course moon periods do, indeed, seem to be bad times for long-range decisions, which almost inevitably seem to go awry as the result. Indeed, the periods seem to be far better for introspection and the breaking of habits or attitudes that are reinforced by normal, everyday patterns or beliefs.

Calculating void-of-course periods can be done easily enough by the astrology student with an ephemeris that contains an aspectarian (such as *Raphael's*) — just find the last major aspect (conj., opp., trine, sq., sex.) before the moon changes sign. For the layman, void-of-course times are available in some astrological calendars and in Neil Michelsen's new astrological ephemeris — for info., write Neil at 129 Secor Lane, Pelham, N.Y. 10803. This is one phenomenon that is more than worth your while to check out.

Lunar cycles, among the shortest of all planetary cycles, also have a long-range interpretation in astrology. This is the cycle of the progressed moon (in secondary progression).

In astrology, secondary progression equates the daily motion of a body after birth with a yearly motion. Thus, the moon, which moves about thirteen zodiacal degrees in one day normally, is considered to move the same amount per year by secondary progression.

So, one full 27½ day cycle becomes stretched over 27½ years. The effects of this very symbolic and mathematically hypothetical cycle are reputed to be largely psychological and emotional. Presumably, by age 27½, the individual will have emotionally traversed all the basic qualities of psychological experience he will know as described by the moon's passage by progression through the various zodiacal signs. All experience after that is a repetition and enlargement of his original pattern of emotional growth.

The effects of the progressed lunar cycle are most felt during the life at its peaks and troughs — that is, at the completion of a full 27½ year cycle and at its half-way point of 13¾ years.

The first half-cycle at age 13¾ is the naturally troublesome period of puberty, which is also marked by a number of other cyclical subdivisions as will be discussed later. For the first time since birth, the progressed moon is making an opposition to its natal place and the emotions within are at odds with themselves, marked by radical mood swings and turnabouts that the opposition would imply.

At 27½, the progressed moon returning to its natal place marks just the opposite — a period of settling in of the emotions. The individual has explored the whole range of emotional qualities and the personality has completed the maturing process of the youthful years.

By the time of the next opposition at about age 41, the individual is again in crisis (aided by some other cycles as well). Suddenly, middle age has arrived, and the emotions again go through upheaval — what have been the life's accomplishments, how to accept oncoming old age and the flight of youth, and the like. It is a very important period for personality growth and the problems it engenders have made that age the second most likely time an individual is likely to commit suicide (next to the teen period).

The next lunar return at age 55 again marks a swing in the opposite direction. By this time the individual has learned to accept coming old age and to enjoy the fruits of his life's labors. By this time he is looked upon by peers as someone of knowledge in his field of endeavor and, rather than just resting on his laurels, he continues on to greater achievements reinforced by a sure confidence in his abilities.

The next, and usually final, lunar phase comes at almost 69 and marks the mixed emotions with which all of us must face death. By this time, most people are aware that death may come at any time even for a healthy individual and that is not an easy thing to live with. For most in this society, retirement is an accomplished fact by this time and their newly achieved uselessness to society mixed with the imminence of the Grim Reaper takes some getting used to. It is the final year of the alloted three score and ten.

Of course, these are just average cycles that affect (or afflict) much of the population in the ways described above. Naturally, specific circumstances often totally alter the expected effects of a cycle — certainly a man who has inherited a million dollars at age 41 tends to worry less about the crisis of middle age, while the dying wino of 55 does not tend to revel in his achievements.

But in general, the cycles of the progressed moon along with other fixed cycles to be discussed later do give a fairly accurate picture of the known psychological growth and crisis periods of the average individual.

But lunar cycles, whether monthly or progressed, are the most immediately noticeable of all cycles in their effect upon animal and human behaviour. The scientific exploration into the biological effects of the moon's rhythms already has been, and will continue to be, the leading edge of factual confirmation of the tenets of astrology.

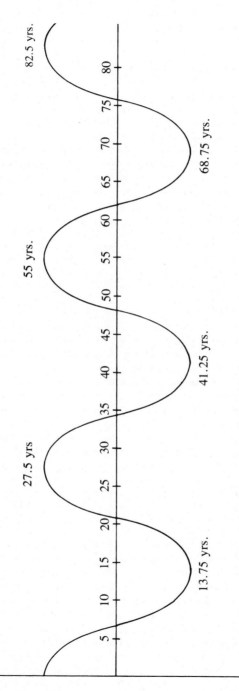

PROGRESSED MOON CYCLE — 27.5 yrs.

Peaks — Emotional assurance, confidence, sense of well-being

Valleys — Emotional low, insecurity, feelings of alienation

13.75 yrs.

27.5 yrs

41.25 yrs.

55 yrs.

68.75 yrs.

82.5 yrs.

Solar Cycles

IF THE SHORTER cycles of the moon are the most noticeable in terms of their effect on human behaviour, the solar cycle is the most critical for the existence of human life itself.

All life on earth depends on the yearly repetition of the solar cycle determined by the earth's revolution around the sun and our planet's inclination to its orbital plane. The seasonal changes thus created determine all the weather, food supplies, and inhabitable topology that enable us to exist at all.

The recognition of our dependency on the sun is deeply imbued in our religious and social customs both ancient and modern.

Logically, the most importance has been given to the beginnings of the four seasons, at which the earth's axis points toward, away from, or is parallel to the sun. Thousands of years before Christ men were building massive stone observatories to determine these times exactly each year. Early man throughout the world held his greatest festivals at the solstices and equinoxes, celebrating the continuance of the cycle that provided life and succor to mankind.

When more modern religions arrived and enshrined this birth-death-rebirth cycle of the seasons into more anthropomorphic terms such as Christian dogma, the religious festivals still kept their dates and thus their integrity at the turn of the seasons.

The winter solstice has seen changes in name — the Roman Saturnalia, Hannukah, the celtic yule festival, and Christmas — but remains the same in spirit. It is still, more than ever, a time of recklessly joyous spending, celebration, and gift-giving, just as in Roman times.

In ancient Rome, the spring equinox marked the beginning of the new year and is currently guised as Easter, (the time of which is determined by the equinox — the first Sunday after the first full moon after the equinox).

The midsummer festival, so dear to the Druids and the medieval English, has resurfaced in this country two weeks later on the Fourth of July (and in France a week before the solstice on Bastille Day).

The fall festival of harvest lingers on in holidays as diverse as Octoberfest, Rosh Hashanah,and Labor Day. The holidays change from generation to generation, but their fundamental solar basis remains the same.

Although the effects of the yearly solar cycle are very obvious to everyone, there is another solar cycle that has only come to light this century. It is the 11-year sunspot cycle.

Every 11 years there is a period of peak sunspot activity followed 5½ years later by a period of relative quiet on the sun's surface. During the peak periods the sunspot areas emit a wide range of intense radio and electromagnetic radiation of various types causing some obvious physical effects on earth such as increased radio interference and heightened displays of aurora borealis and australis, both indicating an increased bombardment of solar radiation to the earth's magnetic envelope.

But apparently these sunspot cycles have biological effects as well. During the 1930's Dr. Miki Takata discovered that the "flocculation index" of human blood serum was affected by the onset of the sunspot cycle peak. In the same decade, it was found that the same cycle significantly altered the growth of tree rings — a discovery that has been more recently put to use by archaeologists in the bristle-cone pine method of historical dating, a cross-check on the older carbon-14 method.

But most interesting is Soviet professor A.C. Tchyivsky's correllation of sunspot cycles with what he calls a human "mass excitement cycle". He found that throughout history events such as wars, migrations, crusades, uprisings, revolutions, etc. seemed to cluster around the peak sunspot periods. In the three years surrounding the peaks he found 60% of such events occurred, while in the troughs of the cycle only 5% occurred.

Such an analysis of historical human behaviour must naturally be colored by the researcher's own view of history, but at any rate it is fairly well accepted that peak sunspot activity does stimulate higher levels of activity in the human, animal, and vegetable kingdoms.

Although studies on the physical effects of the sun's cycles on living creatures are still in the earliest of stages, the astrological effects of that cycle are highly delineated and, in fact, go to make up the fundamental basis for the field. For it is the twelvefold division of that cycle that determines the signs of the zodiac, the lattice upon which all astrological occurrences are laid. The cycles of the moon and all the other planets are assigned significance by being laid upon the field created by the yearly solar cycle, with the beginnings of the seasons marking the foremost, or cardinal, signs.

At first glance, the qualities of the signs seem to fit all too well the seasons they describe in the Northern Hemisphere — Leo being summery, Capricorn being wintry, and the like. If this were strictly the case, the qualities of the signs would be reversed in the Southern Hemisphere and lose their distinctiveness entirely at the equator.

In astrological experience, however, such is not the case. In all forms of astrology — natal, horary, and otherwise — the signs retain their qualities uniformly around the globe.

If not seasonal in origin, what then determines the qualities of the signs? So far it's anybody's guess, but most likely it's a combination of factors. Culturally, the qualities of the signs are certainly influenced by the qualities of the seasons in the Northern Hemisphere, as that is where astrology developed. Astronomically, it could be the relationship of the polar axis to the Galactic Center, a good argument for sidereal astrology or for a changing of the qualities of the signs pursuant to the precession of the equinox. Then again, it could be the varying speed relationship of sun and earth as the two spin around each other orbiting the galaxy, giving a cyclical Doppler-like effect to the radiation striking earth both from the sun and the Galactic Center. There are so many long-range variant factors that there is really no way of telling as yet, since we have only a few thousand years of experience judging the qualities and possibly changeability of the signs.

But working on a less grandiose time-scale, the astrological effects of the solar cycle are both important and unique to each individual, depending on his birth chart. The overall effects fall into two categories, one dependent upon the native's birthday (his natal sun position) and the other dependent on his birth time (determining his ascendant and other house cusps).

The first is the simplest and most general in effect. Since the sun in a birthchart represents primary energy, both physical and emotional, when the transiting sun makes its return to that natal point each year it tends to lend its reinforcement to give the individual energy to burn at that time of year. In fact, a chart cast at the exact time the sun returns to its natal place (the solar return chart) is supposed to give a map of the energy patterns and occurrences of the coming year for the individual. This may vary, but the general effect of the solar return season is one of energy and benificience, perhaps an explanation for recent findings that, statistically, people tend to die shortly after their birthdays, when the energy begins to wane, rather than in the month preceding that date.

Conversely, the time of year opposite the birthday (solar low) is usually the bottoming-out point of the year for an individual. It marks a propensity for fatigue, a low resistance to viruses, and a generally depressing period. Although few astrologers use it, a solar low chart cast for this time seems to reveal a good picture of the down side of the coming year. For those who know to expect it, it's a good time to take the yearly vacation and just lay back for a while.

Naturally, both solar high and low effects are subject to the mitigating effects of the other planetary positions in the natal chart. Those with a large stellium involving the moon opposing the sun may find the solar low more stimulating than the high, for instance.

The effect of the sun's cycle in respect to the ascendant and houses of the birthchart are equally as noticeable, but in a more external and less internal way. Each year, as the sun passes over an individual's ascendant he is likely to find himself more noticed in other's eyes and generally seen in a better and more favorable light than at other times of the year (and the opposite six months later). It is as if the sun acts as a focus of men's minds and when the sun reaches your ascendant, all of a sudden you come to the attention of others whereas you might have gone unnoticed before.

Similarly, when the sun passes over the natal midheaven, the native's reputation and public achievements are brought to the fore. Thus, as a practical application, a person seeking a new job would do well to show up in person if the sun were transiting his ascendant — but if the sun were passing over his midheaven he would be better off sending a resume, for hiring on the basis of achievement rather than personal appearance.

SOLAR CYCLE — 365¼ days

Solar High — Peak physical energy, health, self-confidence

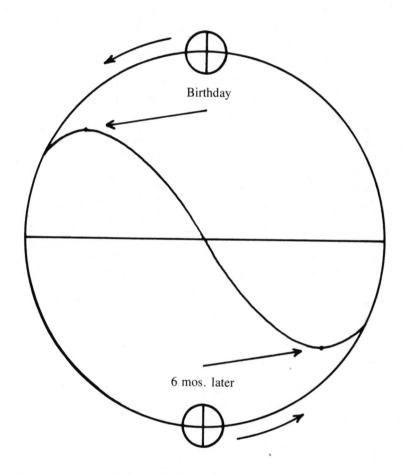

Birthday

6 mos. later

Solar Low — Energy low, weaker health, emotional ebb

Naturally, the interplay of these two cycles yearly can cause anomalies, some amusing, some tragic. The individual born at sunset (sun opposite ascendant) will usually look his best when he feels his worst (sun over ascendant, solar low) and vice-versa. Or the person born at midnight (sun opposite midheaven) will be at his physical worst (solar low) when opportunity knocks (sun to midheaven), thus spending his life behind the scenes, the traditional interpretation of that solar position.

As the sun moves from house to house through the year, it also tends to lend energy to those areas that each house governs traditionally, but more loosely and less noticeably than its effect when near the ascendant or midheaven.

Although these two cycles will vary in the intensity of their effects from individual to individual, the basic phenomena are usually noticeable in everyone.

Knowledge of these basic solar cycles is useful to astrologer and layman alike. It gives a basic energy and opportunity framework around which to plan the year in such a way that one picks the optimum time for self-presentation and knows when to figure on beating a retreat and re-charging energies.

Travelling with the sun in its yearly cycle, as seen from the earth, are the planets Mercury and Venus. Their orbits being interior to that of the earth, they never are seen very far from the sun from the earth's point of view. They serve largely, on a cyclical basis, to reinforce the effect of the sun cycle, but do have effects of their own when they touch, say, the natal sun, ascendant, or midheaven. Because of their varying rates of motion, including retrograde, they may hit the same point twice or more in a season rather than just once. Briefly, Venus will bring favorable looks or events while Mercury will lend intellectual inspiration or clarity of insight — but an analysis of the effects of transits in general are outside the scope of this book.

There is one more important solar cycle that is really the result of another cycle — the 19-year cycle of the motion of the plane of the moon's orbit. It is the solar eclipse cycle and although there are usually at least a couple of partial or total solar eclipses each year, it means that there will usually be an eclipse near the same degree of the zodiac once every nineteen years.

A solar eclipse will have little effect upon an individual unless it occurs upon the degree of one of the planets or the angles of his chart. In that case, it will have the effect of a sudden reversal, or repolarization, of events in the area concerned.

Thus, an eclipse upon a person's ascendant may have the effect of causing him to radically alter his appearance (grow a beard, shave one off, dye the hair, adopt a new style of clothing, etc.) or may be associated with some outside occurrence that causes an appearance change (an accident,

SUN/MIDHEAVEN CYCLE —

Reputation is at yearly high — career energies renewed

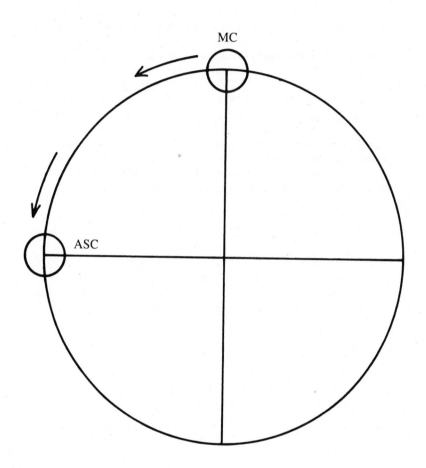

SUN/ASCENDANT CYCLE —

Positive response to personal image — high physical energy

new financial circumstances, etc.). Then, nineteen years later, another eclipse will occur near the same degree and another set of changes will come about.

For the average person this would mean receiving about an eclipse a year on some part of his chart. But few people's charts are statistically average, so most will go for a few years untouched and then get two or three eclipses in a single year which will thus mark a period of marked change for the individual, to be repeated again every nineteen years.

This is not an absolutely strict cycle and may at times shorten to 18 years or lengthen to 20 for an eclipse near the same degree, but it averages nineteen and an ephemeris is best used to determine the exact date of the eclipse as its effects are well worth watching for — and watching out for.

All in all, solar cycles are the most reliable in their predictable effect upon the given individual, just as monthly lunar cycles are the most noticeable among masses of individuals on a short-term basis. The awareness of the solar high and low and the sun's passage over the angles of the birth-chart are probably the most valuable cycles one can know — they can save untold time, energy, and unnecessary grief for the individual who is aware of them.

Planetary Cycles

THERE HAS BEEN little, if any, formal scientific research on the effect of the cycles of the planets upon human behaviour. Most researchers in fields outside of astrology itself consider these bodies to be too far away to have any measurable effect on biological patterns.

To the astrologer, however, these cycles, particularly those of Jupiter and Saturn, are fraught with the utmost significance and outweigh the effects of the sun and moon in their long-range effect both upon the individual and upon humanity at large. They represent the patterns of those external events which shape a person's life in a relatively regular and predictable manner.

Of the six planets whose orbits are exterior to that of earth's (the two interior planets, Mercury and Venus, are part of the sun cycle) only three have cycles short enough to be completed in the normal human lifespan.

The shortest of these is the Mars cycle, with a period of a little under two years (about 23 months). In astrology, the planet Mars represents physical personal energy, and its cycle is thus related to the changing amounts of energy available to the individual over each two-year period and the effects of that energy upon his personal life and career.

The beginning and end of each Mars cycle, when it returns to its natal place in the birthchart, mark a personal peak in energy. This does not simply mean that the individual is feeling more robust or energetic (though that often is so) but that simply more is happening that both requires and stimulates energy outlay.

Thus, the individual often finds it a time of new projects and commitments, often accompanied by higher pay status and the increased responsibility and time/energy expenditure such change of status often requires. Naturally, it is a good time to start a new job or project and, conversely, new jobs and projects just seem to turn up at that time.

At the down side of the cycle, when Mars makes the opposition to its natal place, energies are low and interest in ongoing projects and commitments reaches a low ebb. It's almost as if the enthusiasm for the projects begun at the Mars high have run out and the mind turns toward possible new directions that may be realized when the next high is reached again. To that extent, it is a cycle of interest as well as one of energy.

In astrological career counselling this cycle is particularly noteworthy, as it enables the astrologer to have a better idea of whether a client's current job opportunities are real or whether they will turn out to be transient or illusory in nature.

This fixed Mars rhythm, starting at birth and recurring every two years thereafter, is the most noticeable aspect of the Mars cycle. Mars also has a

21

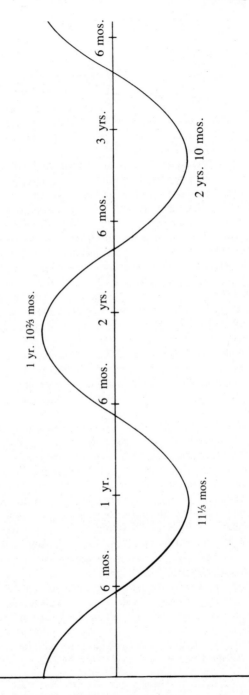

MARS CYCLE — 1 yr., 10⅔ mos.

Peaks — High physical energy, new projects, new jobs, promotions

Valleys — Tired blood, boredom, busywork and/or unemployment

6 mos.

1 yr.

6 mos.

2 yrs.

6 mos.

3 yrs.

6 mos.

1 yr. 10⅔ mos.

11⅓ mos.

2 yrs. 10 mos.

similar two-year cycle based on the times it crosses the ascendant and midheaven (or, for that matter, any of the house cusps), but the effect is more that of a transit rather than a gradual increase and focusing of energy as in the fixed Mars cycle. Thus, one may have a mishap when Mars crosses the ascendant, or a jolt to the career when it touches the midheaven, but there is not the steady buildup and subsequent decline of energies that is marked by the natal Mars return and opposition.

◆ ◆ ◆

Because of its slower speed, Jupiter's effects throughout its cycle are much more pronounced and tangible than those of Mars, not only at its peak and trough but throughout its entire orbit, particularly as it effects the houses of the natal birthchart.

Of first importance, of course, is its fixed cycle in relation to its own natal position — the Jupiter return and opposition, an 11.88-year cycle. Jupiter is associated with all things expansive, outgoing, ebullient and the like, and represents the expansive ego-life principle of the sun as manifested in tangible social directions — career commitments on a large scale (as opposed to smaller intra-career changes such as promotions, moving to a new company, etc.). Its natal position represents, along with all the other planets' positions, the natal commitment to life — the untrammeled child bursting into the unfettered learning experience of the earlier years.

With the first natal opposition at age six, schooling normally begins and the formal restrictions and social fetters are first laid upon the child, the Jupiter energy at its first ebb. But by twelve years of age, puberty has begun, and with it the unavoidable, head-over-heels tumble into adolescent sexuality — new feelings, new situations, a whole new emotional and social ball game.

But by nearly eighteen, the thrills of new-found sexuality and maturity are replaced by the graver duties of earning a living or at least studying full-time to learn a profession — again the Jupiter ebb.

Shortly before age 24 the individual has progressed far enough into youthful maturity to begin personal expansion again or in the case of those previously studying for a profession, the career is launched. At any rate, another Jovian period has begun.

And so it goes, up and down, as long as the life continues. The material effects are different at different ages, particularly as they combine Jupiter cycles with cycles of Saturn and other planets. These combined influences, marking the critical growth periods of life, are discussed in the following chapter.

Jupiter's path through the houses of the natal chart, starting at the ascendant, marks another set of twelve 11.88-year sub-cycles. Each sub-cycle with its high and low mark the periods of maximum and minimum expansion and activity in the matters of the house concerned.

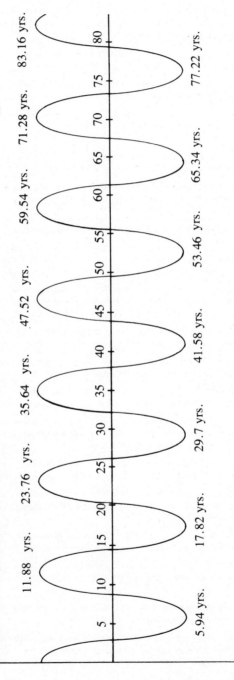

JUPITER CYCLE — 11.88 yrs.

Peaks — High energy, enthusiasm, expansion into new areas of experience

11.88 yrs.   23.76 yrs.   35.64 yrs.   47.52 yrs.   59.54 yrs.   71.28 yrs.   83.16 yrs.

5.94 yrs.   17.82 yrs.   29.7 yrs.   41.58 yrs.   53.46 yrs.   65.34 yrs.   77.22 yrs.

Valleys — Low energy; rest, retreat into established behavior patterns

The Ascendant and First house — As Jupiter passes over the ascendant it tends to bring the personality out of its shell and into the limelight and attention of others. It marks a time of high energy and great activity whenever personal appearances (rather than, say, financial commitments) are concerned. Flamboyance, agressiveness and charisma are at their highest and the individual will find he can make his mark and find acceptance in areas previously shut to him by sheer force of personality. Others will be much more easily convinced that he is an idea whose time has come — not necessarily so much because of his real talents but because his ascendant is the direction in which the world is looking for new expansion and development. This is rather like the effect of the yearly sun cycle to the ascendant — the sign Jupiter tenets acts as sort of a Jupiter-filter for the world, and those with ascendants there look the better for it.

Second house — This marks the peak time of cash-flow for most. If one attains wealth at the time, one has equally the likelihood of spending it as fast as it comes in. Not necessarily wantonly, but merely because circumstances so dictate. It is the most likely time of being self-employed, and the time people will look to you as a well-heeled big spender, even if you're not. It's generally a fun period that passes all too quickly.

Third house — This is brainstorming time, when ideas come burgeoning forth out of the overworked mind. Much of these are excellent thoughts which, though of little value at the time, may have great value later. Therefore, it is a very wise move to jot down all your brilliant little flashes lest they be forgotten by the time they are of use in the coming years.

Fourth house — Likely as not, this is moving day. The year Jupiter spends passing through the fourth house almost invariably finds one moving from one house (or apartment) to another, or at least making radical changes and reworkings (usually improvements and additions) to an already existing abode. In a deeper sense it may mean fortifying your emotional home base, but in the midst of moving furniture one tends to overlook that. Certainly, the emotions are focused inward, even if that only means inside the four walls of your dwelling.

Fifth house — This is the peak period for creativity — songs, poems, paintings, plays, dance and anything which requires a lot of inspiration from the Muse. This need not simply apply to the arts themselves alone. Most every endeavor requires inspiration and creativity to a degree, and so this tends to be a good period for everyone. Pursuits of any nature tend to be more enjoyable during this year, and one also tends to pursue enjoyment and leisure more at this time as well.

Sixth house — Jupiter passing through the sixth tends to send one scurrying off to promote all kinds of projects and generally to take care of business. It's a peak period for the tying up of loose ends, taking care of details, and in general the polishing of the creations of the fifth house period. Not a lot seems to get accomplished or any great projects undertaken, but it's an important time for clearing away and getting potential stumbling blocks out from underfoot.

Seventh house — This is the bottom of the 1st house cycle and a period in which the energy formerly given to oneself is now lavished upon others. It is usually a year in which many new friendships are made and one finds greater concern for the well-being of others than for oneself. It is, in general, a period of socialization and integration of oneself into the general matrix of society in a workable and enjoyable fashion.

Eighth house — Since this is the bottom of the 2nd house cycle, it is usually the period of greatest dependency on others for financial support. That is, the income is usually derived from working on projects other than one's own. It is often a fairly quiet time and one for the restoring and regenerating of used-up energies.

Ninth house — The bottom of the 3rd house cycle, words do not come easy but ideas and general concepts do. One tends to make commitments one is not quite ready to fulfill in reality. It's rather like a car freshly started on a cold morning — it's a good time for warming up and gathering together of directions, but quick starts are ill-advised.

Tenth house — This is the peak of the Jupiter cycle for new plans and expansion in career matters which, naturally, are the concern of the 10th house. Others tend to look well on your proposals and generally think highly of you. The only stumbling block is that this favorable filter may be somewhat illusory and after Jupiter passes this peak the same ideas may seem not half so prepossessing. It is also the bottom of the 4th house cycle, so inward attentions and cares are neglected as the energies turn outward to impress the public.

Eleventh house — As the bottom of the 5th house cycle, it is a period of relying for creativity upon others — leaning on your well-placed connections, to use an old 11th-house keyword. If the previous year's career exploits were half what they seemed at the time, one's reputation leads to a more profitable set of circumstances — a period of personal and financial exploitation of one's previous efforts.

Twelfth house — The bottom of the 6th house cycle, instead of rushing about picking up details, the personality is either dormant or at work behind the scenes preparing for the coming ascendant peak cycle. It is also a time of maximum psychic energies and the most likely time to personally experience psychic phenomena of one sort or another.

Jupiter-sun cycle — One other particularly noteworthy Jupiter cycle is that of its transiting conjunction and opposition to the natal sun. At the conjunction end the physical energies are at a peak and the individual tends to simply throw himself into every available project and commitment — a time of boundless energy and optimism, but one which can lead to serious overcommitment and overwork, leading to financial and physical ill-health. It is best to go easy and move with the available energy rather than to exploit it too aggressively.

Conversely, at the bottom of the cycle there is very little energy or self-motivation available. The inclination is to sit back and let the world go by — not a bad idea, but again not to be overdone, lest opportunities needlessly

SATURN CYCLE — 29.42 yrs.

Peaks — High degree of social dependency, social integration & conformity

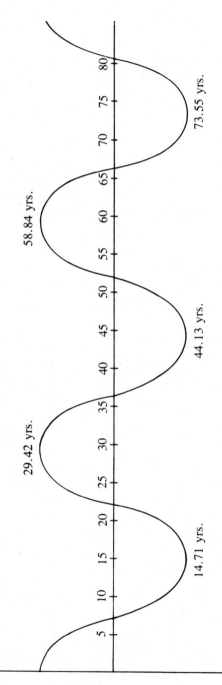

Valleys — Low social integration, high individuation, social separation, non-conformity

pass you by. Simple awareness of the cycle will enable one to avoid the excesses to which the Jupiter cycle high and low points are inclined.

Similar effects may be noted at the Jupiter conjunction and opposition to the natal moon, but they are generally not nearly so pronounced and tend to be active more in the emotional than the physical life — e.g., an overabundance of emotional reactions at peak and an emotional drought at opposition.

◆ ◆ ◆

Of all planetary cycles, however, that of Saturn is probably the most important — particularly to the astrologer, as it is the effects of this cycle that provide him with most of his business. Normally few people will consult an astrologer unless they are under some kind of duress that cannot be explained by other means, and that duress is usually the result of one aspect or another of the Saturn cycle. Many look upon Saturn with a jaundiced eye, but astrologers should avow particular affection for it, as without it the astrology profession would most likely perish.

The Saturn cycle is the longest that most people are likely to see completed in a lifetime — 29.42 years. Whereas Jupiter represents the outgoing, expansive principles in life, Saturn portrays the opposite — constriction, retention, deprivation, and crystalization. Its immediate effects are generally unpleasant, but its long-range effects tend to favor stability and the accumulation of wealth and security. In its worst aspect it symbolizes the imprisonment of the individual by outside circumstances — at its best it represents the integration of the individual within the environmental and social order.

The Saturn cycle reaches its first low (transiting Saturn opposite natal Saturn) just before age fifteen (14.71). In the Jupiter-begun(at 12) throes of adolescence, the individual is externally at his most anti-social and internally at his least personally integrated. It is certainly the most difficult period for the parents, who are the child's main Saturnizing influence, and for his teachers also. It is equally as hard for the child who, in the process of establishing his own independent identity, cuts himself off from the comforts of his previously secure existence. It is usually the time of maximum alienation and its resulting problems — dropping out, drugs, delinquency, and suicide.

Gradually, in most cases the personality comes to terms with the pressures and demands of society, reaching a peak of new-found stability at the Saturn return at age 29½. This is for the majority an age of settling-in to career, home and family. The tumult of early youth is past, middle age and its agonies are safely in the future, and the time is usually one of earnest and enjoyable efforts to establish and build upon an increasingly stabilized life situation. It is this first favorable breath of Saturn that banks the fires of youth and politically tends to swing everyone a bit more to the right.

The next low point of the Saturn cycle comes at age 44 and is the last in a series of cycle lows beginning at 40. It is likely to find the individual feeling very middle-aged and out of touch with society in general. In women, the problem is aggravated by menopause as well, and for all it is usually the last step in the second major life crisis (the first being adolescence) and is accordingly accompanied by a steep rise in the suicide rate. It is the time that one must, of necessity, build a new relationship with oneself and the world at large, as youth and its goals have flown and a revised set of purposes must be devised and heartfully adopted.

But by almost 59 the whole story has reversed itself again and the Saturn return, aided by other positive cycles, again finds the individual emotionally reintegrated with society and, for most, at the final full flower of life. The fruits of a lifetime are usually on the table and the ability to make more is still in hand, resulting in a feeling of accomplishment and confidence. And, since the fruits of accomplishment appear to have been the result of successful policies of the past, the political inclinations again tend to shift toward the right, generally in proportion to the apparent success attained, thus accounting for a lot of rich old Republicans.

Most of us do not survive the long slide down to the next Saturn low at age 73. For most it marks the end of a reburst of energy sparked by a Jupiter return at 71 and a withdrawal from society — the harbinger of death.

Of course no astrological cycle by and of itself can make anyone kick the bucket, but by the seventies a combination of infirmity, social uselessness, and astrological energy lows are enough to plant all but the staunchest in their graves. But if the more fortunate and sprightly manage to make it past the Jupiter low at 77, they can expect a host of very positive high-energy cycles to peak after 80 and they may get a whole new lease on life. Astrologically, life begins again at 80. . .

Saturn's 29½ year transit cycle to the natal houses is probably the most important of any planetary cycle in terms of its long-range effect upon the security and stability of an individual's life. Symbolically, Saturn is the dues-payer and the solidifier of circumstance — as it circles the chart it crumbles the weaknesses of whatever area it touches and allows only what is strong and enduring to remain. Its first effects are those of withering and testing, its final result a more stable, if somewhat smaller, edifice. It blows away the chaff and lets the wheat remain or, to be even more Biblical, it turns the adversities of youth into the bulwarks of old age. In the short run it is restrictive and destructive, in the long run it is creative and evolutionary.

Saturn tends to have a rather poor reputation among astrologers, as it is the cause of most of their clients' woes, but when looked at from a cyclical point of view it must be considered in its most positive light or the knowledge of it will be one of watchfulness rather than utility. Saturn's cycles are the most useful of any planet and those who shrink from taking advantage of it are unfortunate indeed. Little of lasting value can be won without contest and those who avoid challenge can find little substantive reward.

Which is not meant to imply that one should not take precautions upon the arrival of important Saturn transits, but in order to benefit from them it is important to meet them head on. Simply withdrawing ahead of time to avoid possible difficulties only serves to leave untested those means and abilities that one will need to rely on to meet future and perhaps less avoidable challenges.

The first house — Saturn's passage over the ascendant and through the first house marks a testing period for the personality and will power of the individual. It often seems like you're going about with a great weight upon your shoulders. It is a time of personal challenge and confrontation by others, when the limits of your personal authority will be tested and established for the coming 29½ years. It is often a time of physical strain, but more as a result of emotional drain than actual physical burden or injury.

The second house — This period will mark the establishment of budgetary habits and customs — the manner in which you govern the flow of money and property through your domain. At first the effect is one of real or impending impoversihment, pointing up the need for a better system of control and retention of funds. Ideally, the final result is the less wasteful and more efficient use of personal assets and a set of habits governing them that will stand up to trial in the future.

The third house — This is the period of trial and establishment of your ideas and techniques of getting things done. It will shape the style and manner in which you practice your profession. It also tends to mold the outward personal style — those details of personal mannerisms that will identify you to others for many years to come. Excessive flamboyance is trimmed and modes of personal expression become more succinct, forming a skeleton to build upon for the rest of the cycle.

The fourth house — This often marks a period of greater attention to career than to the home, which is cut back through necessity and circumstance to a bare minimum. One learns just how much, and no more, is needed for the necessary privacy and retreat to keep the soul fires burning. At best it is a time of efficiency of living, at worst it can become a mere neglect of the home and the subsequent decay thereof. If properly exploited, it will show you just how little you can get along with and still make a house a home.

The fifth house — The most noticeable effect of Saturn here is a significant lessening of the sexual drive. This, however, is just a reflection of the holding back of 5th house matters in general. It is a very uncreative period artistically, but it also is a lesson on getting along without your Muse, who just can't be at your beck and call twenty-four hours a day. In general, it offers the opportunity to learn profitable alternatives or substitutes for play, whether sexual or artistic, which will shore up the personality in the future when the Muse (or the lover) is out to lunch.

The sixth house — This is a period of finding out just how little work one can get away with and still suffice. Not so much out of laziness, but because there is too much to do and you cannot spend the time on details that would be desired. Quality is inclined to falter despite all effort, but it is the test of just how much can be managed at once without breaking down, a period of maximizing stamina and staying power to be used in the future.

The seventh house — As the bottom of the first house cycle, this is a period of trying the defensive, rather than the aggressive, perimeters of the personality. Its primary concern is with others and establishing just how much they may be allowed to impinge upon and control your own interests. For those involved in close partnerships such as marriage a rebalancing takes place putting the relationship on a more equal and functional level, often resulting in a split for those whose partnership was not properly stable to begin with.

The eighth house — This is a period of learning to use the resources of others to your own ends and to budget them so that you may continue to receive outside help in your ventures. As the bottom of the 2nd house cycle, it means you may have your own resources in good shape, but you must rework others' efforts in order to get what you want. The keyword for this is probably *manipulation,* hopefully in as honest and pleasant a way as possible. Your abilities to convince others that what you want is really what they want will be tried and tested — a useful talent to have at all times. On the higher side, it is a period of simplification of philosophical life views, particularly those concerning death, that may tend toward over-simplification but will provide a basis for building upon later.

The ninth house — This is a period that may be called *principleless* in a manner of speaking. Since Saturn tests the character by deprivation and the 9th house is associated with general principles and moral justifications in general, it represents a test of the ability to live life just for itself alone with a minimum of moral or physical controls and motivations. It lets you realize, as much and as purely as you will for a long time to come, how little goal-orientation can mean to the human animal. As the down side of the 3rd house cycle, it avoids formality or crystalization of expression and the mind tends to drift and ramble more than at most other parts of the cycle.

The tenth house — Saturn passing over the midheaven and through the tenth house naturally tends to make career efforts more of a struggle and the world at large hears less of them, whatever their quality. Success may be had more easily in Saturnine areas — older, more traditional professions, established companies, and the like. It is the time to learn to live with a minimum of fanfare and reputation and to concentrate upon quality. As the bottom of the 4th house cycle, it inclines one to withdraw to the protection of home, either literally or figuratively.

The eleventh house — The lesson of this cycle is in learning to make a little outside help go a long way. It is a time of dearth of good outside connections and support from higher up, so every drop of assistance must be parlayed into a bucketful single-handedly in order to suffice. Naturally, after being little or not well heard of during the 10th house cycle, outside support is likely to be scarce, so it is a further period of self-reliance. But as the down side of the Saturn 5th house cycle, there should be enough creativity to provide a basis of self-reliance.

The twelfth house — This period is about the most difficult to learn from, as 12th house experiences are the mot difficult ones to nail down. Certainly there is less psychic experience and support and it is also the period for the development of those forces that will oppose you openly when Saturn reaches the ascendant. Sadly, it is a wise time to be suspicious of friends and a good time to make sure all commitments are set down in writing and signed, lest you find yourself later betrayed with no evidence to support you. As the bottom of the 6th house cycle, work may be scarce but what there is of it will be easy. But in all, it is best put as a time to learn to use your suspicions wisely. Enemies are afoot, even if they themselves do not know it.

Of note as well are the cycles marked by the transit of Saturn to the natal sun and moon. As it crosses the sun the period of peak strain on the inner energies is reached, often marked by simply too many things to do and the resulting drain of sufficient energies to put into each thing. Conversely, the bottom of the cycle may find you rather lazy, with energy to waste and nowhere to put it. As Saturn transits the moon, the strain is more emotional, often with those around you putting the pressure on, while at the bottom of the cycle you wish someone would pay you more attention.

Throughout, the lesson of the twelve Saturn house-cycles is one of learning to function at one's best with a minimum of support in any one area. It is a bother and a pain at first, but it teaches economy and efficiency, without which we should waste all our resources with little effect. When Saturn passes from a house, it leaves that area trimmed to the bone, a minimum of structure with a maximum of effectiveness. Then, the ensuing two passes of Jupiter will reforest the area at first filling it out and eventually overcrowding it in preparation for another trimming from Saturn 5½ years later. Neither Saturn nor Jupiter cycles should be looked at alone, but as the two balancing factors in the growth and health of the personality and its circumstances.

Similarly, each house-cycle peak should not be looked at as a solo occurrence every so many years. It is merely the greatest intensity of certain types of events that continue to happen at varying intensities throughout the rest of the cycle. A cycle peak is less of an event than a concentration of certain trends that are ordinarily active to a greater or lesser extent at all times.

◆ ◆ ◆

The only other planetary cycle that is at all likely to be completed in a lifetime is the Uranus cycle of approximately 84 years. Although most of us won't see one completed, and therefore cannot take advantage of the experience of one cycle to benefit the next, it still has a measurable effect on the overall life-pattern and is therefore worthy of note.

The Uranus cycle is essentially a life-discovery cycle. It is at its peak at birth, like all other cycles, the first and probably most startling experience any of us go through. It then continues to decline until age 42 when most find themselves having pretty well mined out life's novelties. That age is a crisis period as it is the bottom of four different cycles, but once past and a new outlook on life is developed the individual has a second lease on life and freshness and discovery again seem a possiblity.

On the difficult side, it is a cycle of restlessness and social troublesomeness as well. The individual is at his most socially unintegrated before the age of 21 and after the age of 63, the times when the Uranus cycle is closer to its peak than its bottom. Between those ages, the individual's efforts are more closely linked with those of the society around him — before and after those ages the interests of the individual are increasingly more self-centered and less those of the society at large. In essence, the Uranus cycle represents the degree to which a person is centered upon his own individuality and its importance as opposed to the needs and demands of the social matrix surrounding him.

Thus, at its peak (rarely seen except in childhood or, perhaps, "second childhood") the individual on the positive side has a very high sense of self-worth but on the negative side is most uncooperative when it comes to the needs of others. At its bottom, the individual is a real cooperator socially but also may go through a crisis of seeming personal unimportance and worthlessness.

Of course, as with all cycles, this is only a social generality. Some people are simply mavericks all their lives while others seem to blend into the background from the day they are born, depending upon the individual.

Passing through the houses of the individual natal chart, Uranus simply has the effect of a transiting body, since its positions will never be repeated to form a growing cycle pattern. As is known with Uranus transits, the affairs of each house it passes through will tend to undergo tumultuous changes for the duration and the period marks the maximum time of self-discovery in those areas, but it will not recur again in a lifetime, and some houses in most individual's charts will never be touched at all.

The same is true with Neptune, as most persons will not survive even one-half of its cycle. It represents in an overall fashion the continual lessening of idealism and blind, unquestioning faith that occurs throughout the life, beginning its real downswing at about 41, adding to the general middle-age emotional crisis.

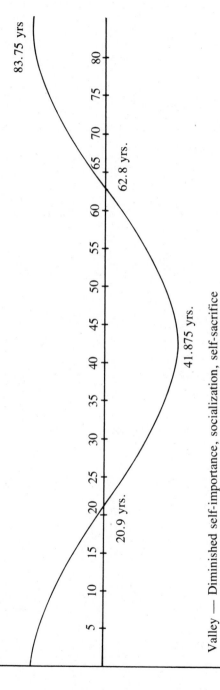

URANUS CYCLE — **83.75 yrs.**

Peaks — self-discovery, self-differentiation

83.75 yrs

62.8 yrs.

41.875 yrs.

20.9 yrs.

Valley — Diminished self-importance, socialization, self-sacrifice

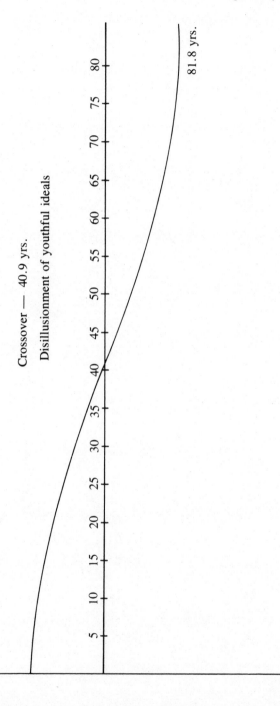

NEPTUNE CYCLE — 163.74 yrs.

Crossover — 40.9 yrs.

Disillusionment of youthful ideals

81.8 yrs.

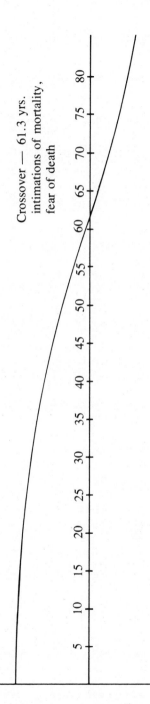

PLUTO CYCLE — 245.33 yrs.

Crossover — 61.3 yrs.
intimations of mortality,
fear of death

The Overall Life-Cycle

THE NEXT LOGICAL step after inspecting the nature of the different individual planetary cycles is to see if, when put together, the total sum comes to some sort of workable overall life-cycle or set of life-rhythms.

The easiest way to view this is to put all the planetary cycles on a graph and see where their peaks and bottoms touch or roughly coincide with one another. Any regular inter-cyclical patterns might be looked upon as overall life-patterns.

The results, when the length of the graph is that of the longest cycle one may expect to survive (the Uranus cycle), are startling.

A regular and completely symmetrical graph is produced that describes not only the interlocking patterns of mere planetary cycles, but describes the growth and crisis periods generally accepted by psychologists and philosophers alike.

Most apparent in the combined graph are peaks at 29 and 59 and bottoms at 15, 42 or 43, and 68. Overall, the graph is bilaterally symmetrical with its central point at age 42-43. This is the bottom of all the cycles and is probably the most discouraging time of life for most people as it marks the end of youth's aspirations and the necessary beginning of the reoriented goals of older age.

But what is particularly interesting is that this period is called *middle age*. But the middle of what? If the average age of death is around 65, then this is way past the middle — in fact, the life is almost two-thirds gone. And if one's increasingly swift perception of the passage of time is to be considered (childhood seems to take forever when you're a kid, but time seems to fly as you pass your prime) then you're practically over the hill by the time so-called "middle age" is reached.

What, then, is "middle age"? In our philosophical perception it is the center between youth and old age and in actual fact it is the center of a graph of psychological and correlated planetary periods. Whether or not one manages to live to the ripe old age of 84, one's psychology is centered upon that hypothetical lifespan, if one is to take the concept of "middle age" seriously, as most people do.

But if life is psychologically bisected at age 42, is living after that age some kind of backwards mirror of existence previous to that age? Catch-phrases such as "second childhood" are uneasy suggestions that such might be the case — it is hardly encouraging to think that one begins life with an empty head only to end up with an addled pate for a finale, with a heavy bout of depression in between.

Although that surely has symbolic application, routine inspection reveals that such is not really the case, despite the neat symmetry of the thought. The individual continues to grow and develop throughout all the cyclical ups and downs — only when looked at on a graph does the end of life repeat the beginning, though at times we get the feeling that we've been through all this before.

But by combining all the planetary cycles we may derive an overall life-cycle graph that describes when several cycles peak or bottom together, thus causing generally high or low periods in life.

The first high period runs from birth to about age three. It is the time when the child is strictly concerned with himself and all energies are turned on finding out what he can do with his senses and faculties. It is a period of the untrammelled personality (the only completely free time for the ego) and ends with the beginning of the down side of the first Jupiter cycle.

The next period, from age 3 to 9, bottoming at 6, is the child's first experience with socialization. It requires severe limiting of the ego in order to get along with the social environment and its most difficult point is age 6 when school begins, at which time the first Jupiter cycle is at its low and Saturn also begins the low portion of its cycle.

By age 9 the child has got a pretty good grip on how to handle himself in a socially acceptable manner and still get what he wants. This is the best part of childhood for most and represents the Jupiter high which peaks at almost age twelve.

But despite the elation that Jupiter gives to this period, the Saturn and progressed moon cycles are heading for bottom and once the Jupiter high begins to wane the personality comes down with a crash. Adolescence and puberty heap all kinds of difficulties on the individual, causing everything from alienation and depression to acne by the bottom of the cycle at age 15.

Then ensues a long struggle while the individual strives to get his head above the problems and responsibilities handed him while a teenager. Jupiter, Saturn, and progressed moon cycles are all at their lows, and life seems like pretty much of an uphill climb.

Finally, at age 21, the individual begins a 13-year period of cycle highs during which he establishes himself a place in society — stakes his claim in the world, so to speak. It is the focus of the creative life energies, the flower of youth.

At 21 and just after Jupiter, Saturn, and progressed moon are into their high periods and, just as important, Uranus begins its down cycle. The individual has begun a period of creative socialization in which the personality is expressed by actively blending with society (Jupiter and Saturn) rather than by separation from or opposition to it (Uranus).

After 24, the Jupiter cycle begins to fall off but the Saturn and progressed moon continue to rise until between 27 and 29, at which time the individual is usually most likely to settle down into a regular life routine, accepting the

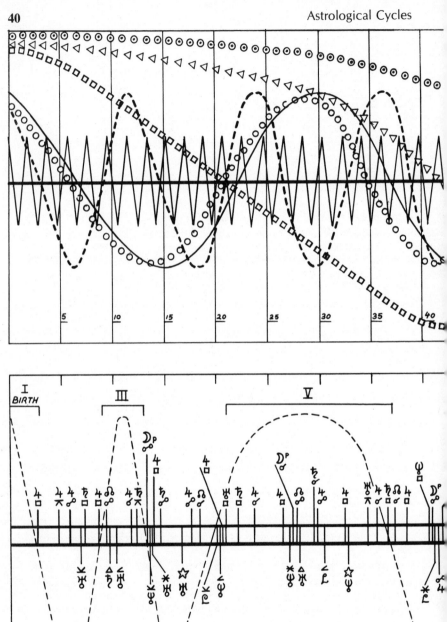

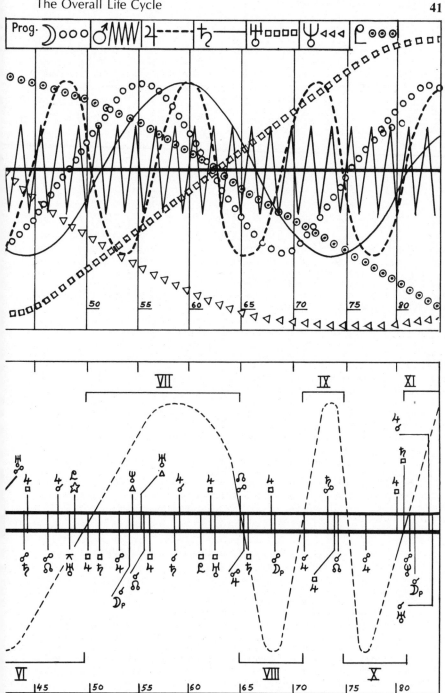

niche that society has provided him rather than carving out new territory,as Jupiter is by that time at its low. For many, it is the first time of rest and security, accompanied by a feeling of havinng established oneself in life.

But as the early thirties pass, Jupiter again peaks and Saturn is headed down, leading to a restless period as the thought of middle age approaches. By 37 or 38 the next low period has begun and by age 42 has usually precipitated the first really important personality crisis since the throes of adolescence.

At 42-43 every planetary cycle is at its low. Middle age has arrived and the attitudes and goals of youth no longer have relevance to the personality. The individual must forge a whole new set of values and objectives that will serve and satisfy a much-changed person. The question of "what have I done with my life" must be answered and a reorientation towards often more meaningful though less physical goals takes place. It is a time of physical and hormonal change for both men and women, and, similar to adolescence, new ways of coping with body and mind must be developed in addition to learning the new social role of the older person. Most go into the period feeling that life is sheer drudgery — the world has passed them by and stranded them in the doldrums. Once new goals and standards have been developed, however, the personality is born anew and, by 50 or so, greets the world with a more cheery, if also more wrinkled, face.

The Jupiter return at 47½ marks the beginning of the end of the long middle-age low period. The rising Saturn and progressed moon cycles bring up the rear and nudge the personality into the next, and for most the final, high period.

The years from 50 to 65 see the individual at the height of his life achievements. This peaks with the mutual Jupiter and Saturn returns at age 59. The combination of mature strength and experience usually bring him substantial effectiveness and respect in his field of endeavor. He lives out those principles and achieves those goals forged in the foundry of middle age, just as the struggles of adolescence led to the achievements of the 20's and 30's.

But as this period begins its downswing after 60 the spectre of death begins to loom large and we all begin preparations to meet our Maker. The real gloom sets in at 65 and continues on until almost 71. This is the time most people die, statistically, and everyone starts thinking about it.

Already, at 62, Uranus has entered into its high cycle and just as the individual enters into society when Uranus starts to swing low at 21, now the personality begins to make preparations for disconnecting from society.

For most, retirement starts at 65 and their cutoff from the social mainstream begins. Thoughts dwell on the past or on impending disease and bodily failure and the personality drifts further from the general social concerns and more toward the personal, individual needs.

But, curiously, those who manage to pass the magical threescore and ten so often seem to experience a new-found elation. They've beat the odds and are living on more time than tradition has alloted them. The Jupiter return at 71 raises spirits and often leads to new friends and involvements previously avoided for fear of a sudden cutoff by imminent death.

But by this age, another factor must be taken into account — illness and impairments it creates. Just as an untoward crippling accident can make the finest peak period of youth a total disaster, so the infirmities of old age tend to dampen and alter the natural cyclical rhythms of life. As one passes 70, the peaks just aren't as peaky anymore and the valleys tend to seem bottomless. Thus the natural peak at about 72 may seem less enthralling than its mirror-image counterpart at age 11 or 12, but the rhythm is still present.

By 75, all cycles except Uranus are down and there ensues a period of quietude and often withdrawal. Both this and the previous period are often called "second childhood — partially because of the common onset of "child-like" senility, but also because the concerns of the individual have turned away from society at large and focused upon himself again as they did in childhood. The Uranus factor, both in its guise of self-discovery and of un-cooperativeness, is on the increase.

But once past 80 or so the personality frequently is on the rise again, culminating in the Uranus return at nearly 84. Despite the ravages of age, it is a period of renewed youth and effort as all the cycles rise — witness the energy of greats like Bertrand Russel and Marc Edmund Jones at this period.

Naturally one could go on, extrapolating future cycle-periods for a being whose incarnate period exceeded that of man, but further speculation about possible cyclical experience of the soul after death and other mystic phenomena are of little use here. Very few live past their mid-80's, and the neat symmetry of the life-graph enclosed by the Uranus cycle is temptingly whole and does not bear disturbing until modern medicine manages to extend our potential physical lifetime by replacing our aging bodies with bionics. We have here a well-tempered pattern that seems to go a long way in describing, if not explaining, the ups and downs of the average lifetime.

And it is well for the astrologer to take these overall periods into careful account when trying to analyze the nativity and current state of any individual. The psychologist has already noted these growth and crisis periods through relatively objective observation, but the astrologer, in whose lap these cycles must fall, has all too often ignored them in favor of the more entrancing and beguiling momentary transits to the natal chart. For all the exciting and tumultuous events that various combinations of planetary transits may describe, they are all etched upon the fundamental underpinnings of the astrological life-cycles that each individual shares with all other human beings of his age.

The overall graph of life-cycles divides the lifetime into 11 periods, the symbology of which may be pleasing both to the astrologer and numerologist:

1. Age 0-3 — Primary individuation, the establishment of the ego and its dominion over the senses and faculties.

2. Age 3-9 — The beginning of socialization and learning to take into account the existence of others and their needs and demands.

3. Age 9-13 — The mastery of internal and external means of success and communication and learning within the protected framework of childhood.

4. Age 13-21 — The testing period in which the individual faces the

problems of becoming an adult and forms the foundation for the life style and personality.

5. Age 21-37 — The establishment of the individual's place in the world, the exercise of one's maximum freedom and creativity.

6. Age 37-50 — The bottom of the life. The period of seeming worthlessness that begets a newer self-image and better overall grip on the world.

7. Age 50-64 — The prime of life, where achievements and reputation join to make the individual both create and at the same time enjoy the fruits of life's physical and spiritual labors.

8. Age 65-71 — The time of death and coping with its necessities. The beginning of withdrawal from the mainstream of society.

9. Age 71-75 — Temporary rejuvenation after escaping expected death. New projects and social exploration.

10. Age 75-81 — Social withdrawal and reevaluation of society's imposed values. Retreat and introspection.

11. Age 81+ — Reassertion of the pure ego, discrete from society's regulation. Rejuvenation of the spirit of and by itself.

Naturally, this rather extended life-cycle does not follow precisely true to course in any individual. The specific vagaries of experience may cause a normally low period to be unusually eventful or creative or a high period to seem quite unmanifested. But as an overall pattern of average human behavior and development this combined life-cycle graph is quite accurately descriptive, coinciding with the psychological crisis patterns recently so popular in the psychiatric profession.

And for the astrologer these patterns will frequently provide the explanation for a client's problems when normal transits, progressions, and other standard techniques fail.

Mundane Cycles

IF ASTROLOGICAL CYCLES can be said to influence individual behavior, then there should surely be some argument that such cycles influence the behavior of society and nations as a whole as well.

The study of such influences comprises the field of mundane astrology — not mundane in the sense of trivial, but in its Lain sense, *world* astrology.

This is an area which could and should entail several volumes to cover sufficiently. Many authors, both astrological and non-astrological, have written extensively upon the subject.

Essentially, astrological mundane cycles fall into two categories: cycles which are simply the period of one planet itself (e.g., Saturn's 29.42 yrs.) or cycles which are the synodic periods of two planets, the time from one conjunction to the next (e.g., the Jupiter-Saturn synod of about 20 yrs.).

Here are some of the more noticed mundane cycles, in order of their length (a by no means complete list of the dozens of possible and postulated cycles).

◆ ◆ ◆

Mars-Uranus cycle — The conjunction of Mars and Uranus occurs every two years. It is traditionally associated with the occurrence or cessation of revolutions, wars, violence, and civil strife. It is perhaps of note that every war the U.S. has ever been involved in has ended within a month of the Mars-Uranus conjunction (with the exception of WW I, where the span was 2½ mos.).

According to certain Australian astrologers, the location of such civil strife in each cycle may be ascertained by determining where on earth the exact conjunction occurs at the midheaven. A band several hundred miles wide on either side of that longitude will contain the major locations of world strife for the 2-yr. period.

I have found this to be quite accurate and have also found that major strife occurs at the longitude of the rising conjunction as well, which troubles usually precede those associated with the midheaven conjunction.

The Jupiter cycle — This is associated with social and aesthetic innovation. It describes increasing waves of social liberalism and, by sign, will often describe the main directions and styles of the popular arts (e.g., regular folk-music revivals each time Jupiter is in Aquarius.). Socially and artistically, new ground broken is a further step upon advances made just 12 years earlier.

The Jupiter-Saturn cycle — The conjunction of Jupiter and Saturn occurs approximately every 20 years. It represents the struggle of liberal and conservative social forces and also may describe great world political and military struggles, as in the period of late 1939-40 during the Battle of Britain. Also of note is that all U.S. presidents inaugurated directly following a Jupiter-Saturn conjunction died in office. The next test of that rule will come for the president that is elected in 1980.

Larger Jupiter-Saturn cycles are considered important as cultural determinants as well. Every 3rd conjunction, which occurs near the zodiacal degree of that 60 yrs. before, is supposed to signify a period of particular upheaval in which the social ideas and innovations of 60 years ago are finally put into effect.

Another important Jupiter-Saturn cycle is the so-called Grand Mutation cycle of 794 years which is supposed to describe the civilization cycle — the time from the birth to the death of an entire culture.

The Saturn cycle — Independent of its relationship with Jupiter, the Saturn cycle is that of social conservatism and rest. As in the case of Jupiter, the manifestations of conservatism at any given time are the outgrowth of similar trends 29½ years ago.

The Saturn-*Uranus cycle* — This has been identified as a weather cycle and a political cycle by some, but of recent curious note is its possibility as a scientific discovery cycle. The Saturn-Uranus conjunction, occurring every 45 years, has marked the years of discovery of the atomic table, radium, the neutron, and the first atomic pile.

The Uranus cycle — Uranus' 84-year period marks revolutionary social change and its acceptance — its ups and downs. Where these changes occur is associated with the sign Uranus tenets. For instance — there appears to be a freedom-repression cycle in sexual matters revolving around Uranus in Scorpio, where sexual aberrations find greatest expression and social tolerance. When Uranus is in the opposite phase in Taurus, sexual conformism is the order of the day and very little deviation from a strict social norm is permitted.

Neptune cycle — Neptune's 164-year cycle is associated most often with religious changes, but again may vary by sign. Neptune in Aquarius, for instance, is quite consistently associated with the great plagues, extending all the way back into Roman times.

Pluto cycle — Pluto is most often connected with death and its cycle socially is associated with the destruction of the established areas of the sign it is transiting, with often devastating effects upon the population associated with the area. Most noticable are the mass migrations (population rebalancing) associated with Pluto in Libra every 245 years and the terrible wars of readjustment that follow as Pluto passes through its own sign of Scorpio. Recent statistics indicate that this is running true to form — there has been more world population migration in the last few years with Pluto in Libra than in the last several hundred. What the 1980's hold with Pluto in Scorpio is anybody's guess.

Neptune-Pluto cycle — This period is associated with religious and religious-cultural genocide, although not at the time of the mutual conjunction necessarily. For instance, working backwards from the wars of the Reformation with Pluto in Aries and Neptune in Aquarius, there were the Crusades, the Christian subjugation of Europe culminating in the Holy Roman Empire, the struggle of Christianity against Rome, and the takeover of the Mediterranean by Rome during the Punic Wars. All were characterized by more than just conquest but by wanton slaughter of those of another religious-cultural persuasion. We have another couple of hundred years to mend our ways before that one repeats itself.

◆ ◆ ◆

Another very long historical cycle is that of the precession of the equinox, not a planetary cycle at all. This is the period in which the drifting equinox which determines our 0° Aries point makes a full circle in relation to the comparatively fixed and distant star background. As the 0°Aries point drifts backward and enters each successive constellatiion, a new age is considered to have begun, characterized by the attributes of the constellation in which it falls.

Thus, during the last two thousand years the 0°Aries point has been in the constellation Pisces, supposedly representing an age of somewhat unenlightened but well-meaning Christian faith sharing the attributes of Pisces and its sorrow-related 12th house.

Currently, the 0° Aries point is entering the constellation Aquarius, heralding the beginning of the much touted ''Age of Aquarius''. The entire cycle takes 25,000 years to return the 0° Aries point to its original place of 2,000 years ago when the signs and the constellations coincided at the birth of modern astrology.

The theory behind this is admittedly weak, but it has been temptingly and sometimes delightfully extrapolated to describe the most sweeping changes in history — most original of which is paleontologist Christine Janis' use of the repetition of the cycle to its fourth order to describe the nature of the evolution of life upon the earth.

There are as many possible mundane astrological cycles as there are combinations of individual planetary cycles added onto eclipse cycles, sunspot cycles, etc., ad infinitum. These are only a few of the more popular — many other less well-known cycles have been correlated with historical patterns, some with very convincing results. Probably the most distinguished researcher in this field is Charles Jayne, and anyone wishing to further investigate the subject in depth should refer to his works, available from the author at 5 Old Quaker Hill Road, Munroe, New York, 10950.

Non-Astrological Cycles and
Other Problems

IT IS THE unfortunate tendency of the unwary astrologer to attribute all happenings in the world to the influences of the planets — a propensity that has earned astrology a very poor reputation in the 20th century.

But the student of cycles will soon find that there are probably more cycles with no relation whatsoever to the heavens than there are planetary-connected ones. A brief perusal of the journal of Pennsylvania's Foundation for the Study of Cycles will reveal that.

Some of these are of little interest to the average person — pig iron cycles, hog price cycles, prairie dog mating cycles, soy bean cycles, and many more too obscure to mention.

Others, however, are interesting, amusing, and sometimes enigmatic. For instance, the weekly human birth cycle peaks on Wednesdays just after midnight and is at a low on Mondays. Or, more puzzling; of those born in New England who live past age two, people born in March may expect to live an average of four years longer than the cycle of people born in July.

According to the FBI city crime rate is 8% higher in February than in the rest of the year, a strange winter peak. However, as might be expected, rape, assaults, and murder peak in the heat of July. Oddly enough, July is the low for negligent manslaughter, which reaches its high in December. Maybe it's the holiday drunk drivers. . .

Some cycles vary from country to country. Male births peak in September in Japan, while Sweden with the same kind of climate shows no such peak.

In the U.S. more famous people and criminals are born during the spring.

The Presbyterian Church reports a 9-year cycle of membership which is the inverse of a 9-year wholesale and common stock price cycle — when prices go down, church attendance goes up. Hmmm.

Dr. Rexford Hersey in research at the University of Pennsylvania with Dr. M.J. Bennett has estalished a 5-week elation-depression cycle in humans. At low periods liver and pituitary functions drop and blood sugar and cholesterol rises. Reportedly 40% of accidents occur at the low 10% of the cycle. Using this theory, the Swiss Air Force (didn't know they had one, did you?) reduced accidents by 80% by grounding trainees during their low period. Apparently there is no way of charting this cycle except to make a day-by-day chart over a period encompassing several 5-week cycles. Presumably the cycle will make itself clear (probably in direct conflict with the aforementioned lunar cycle in chapter two).

Mundane cycles are attributed to other things than the planets as well — most often weather. Some say that civilizations are built during local warming periods that may take hundreds of years, and then die as the weather cools on the downswing. Others attribute the same effects to wet and dry periods, or even allege that combination cycles of heat and humidity determine the rise and fall of democratic societies versus totalitarianism.

Probably the most well-known cycles that owe little to astrology are the popular so-called Biorhythms. These are three differing cycles with physical, mental, and emotional attributes that allegedly begin at birth and continue with complete reguarlity until death. There seems to be no physical basis for these, yet many swear by them and a number of large corporations in Japan use them to reduce accidents in their plants by requiring employees to take paid days off at their low cycles.

Another pitfall for would-be astrological cycle analysts is the rather unreliable specific reliability of cyles in general. A cycle in any area is just a general pattern of regular repetition, but often that is only an overall view. Cycles may skip one or even several turns before reestablishing their rhythms, and such skips may occur at completely unpredictable times, even though the overall cycle keeps stable in the long run. This is hell on would-be future forecasters.

Other cycles that may appear to be planet-related may actually be the result of some other regularly occurring phenomena. The planets do not have an exclusive on their periodicity.

Such a cycle mystery occurred in the research of Dr. E.G. Brown, a physicist and director of Australia's Radio Astronomy Lab. He discovered that regular heavy rainfall could be expected on certain days every year in Australia and throughout the Southern Hemisphere. Similar heavy rain days occurred a few days earlier in the Northern Hemisphere. Was this a solar weather cycle?

Probably not. Further exploration revealed that it was more likely the intersection of the earth's orbit with a cloud of fine meteoric dust. The dust serves as seed particles for raindrops and the date differentiation between Northern and Southern Hemispheres is explainable by a slant in the angle of the cloud as it intersects the earth's orbit. A physical explanation for what might at first have seemed to be an astrological cycle.

But nevertheless, debunkers be damned, there *are* many clear and increasingly accepted astrological cycles that siginificantly effect our behaviour and environment.

Careful study and observation of such cycles will not deliver the future to us on a platter, but they will increase our knowledge of what makes us tick and what in general to expect from ourselves as we pass through life. To ignore these basic life-rhythms which have been recognized by all earlier cultures and religions would be a disservice to the objective "scientific method" which our current culture espouses. It can only be be hoped that the full attention of modern science may be turned to the investigation of such phenomena so that they may be re-expressed and understood in the light of modern technology and again be of meaningful use and value to mankind.